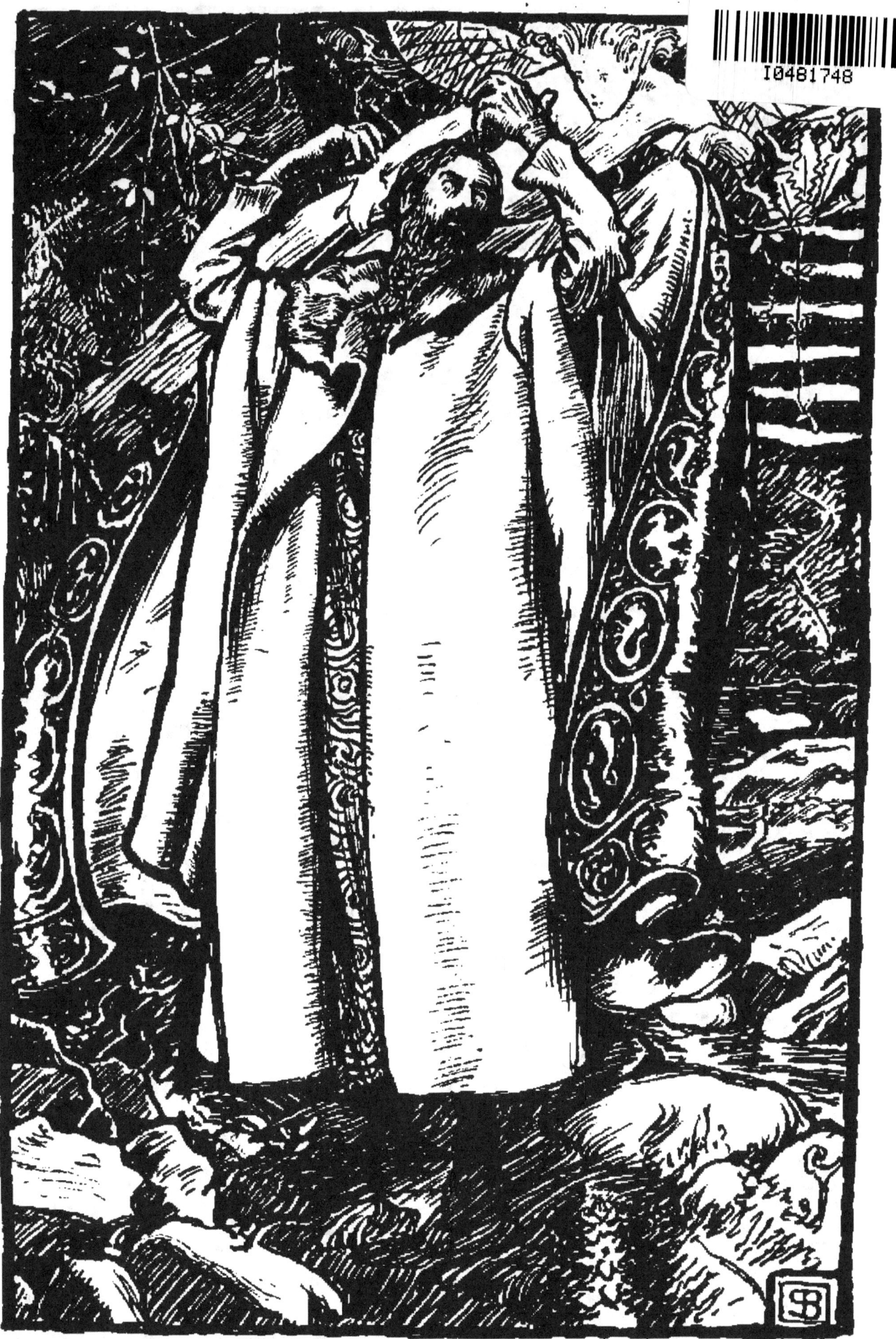

PROSPERO AND ARIEL.

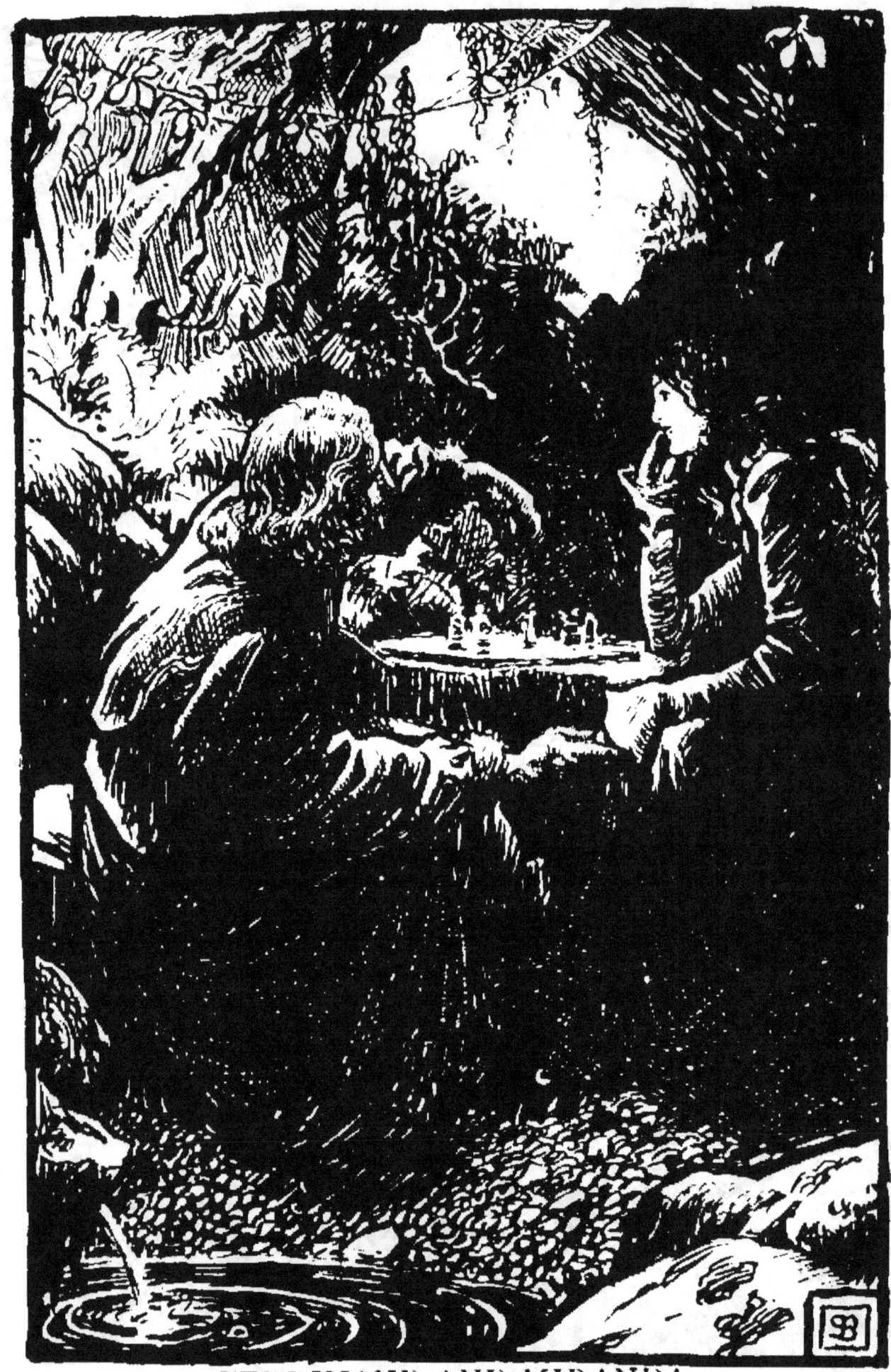

FERDINAND AND MIRANDA.

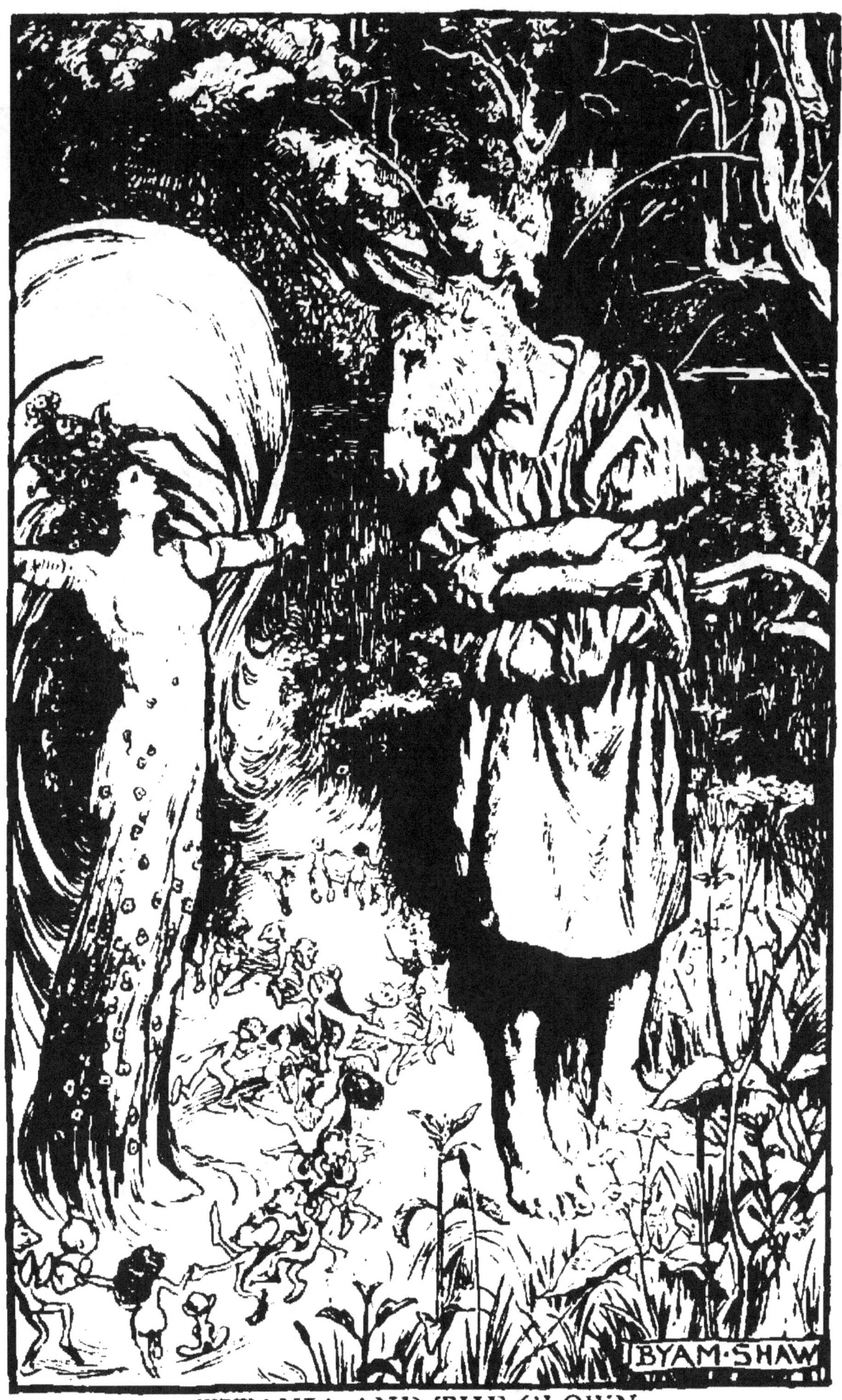

TITANIA AND THE CLOWN.

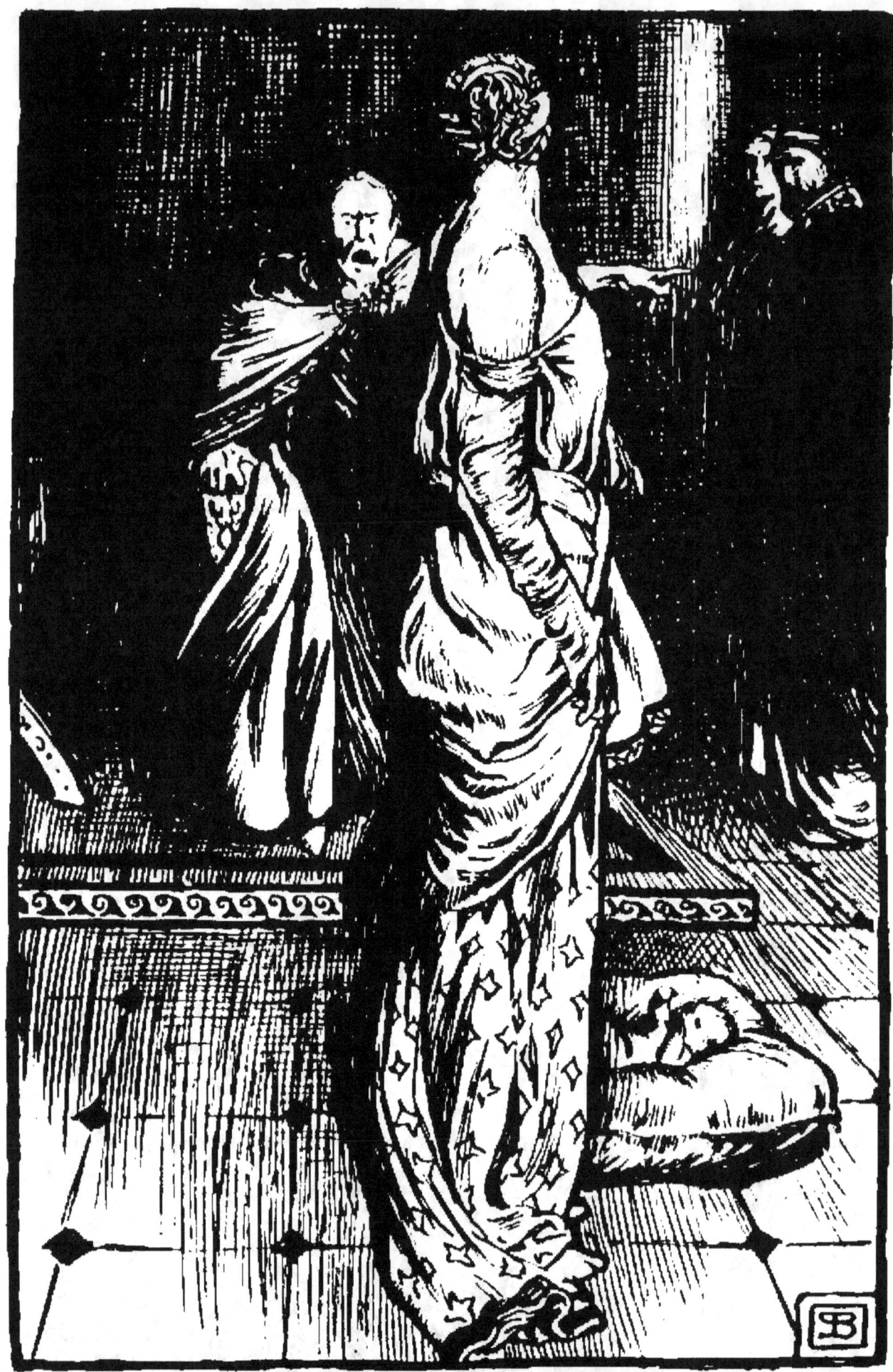

PAULINA AND LEONTES.

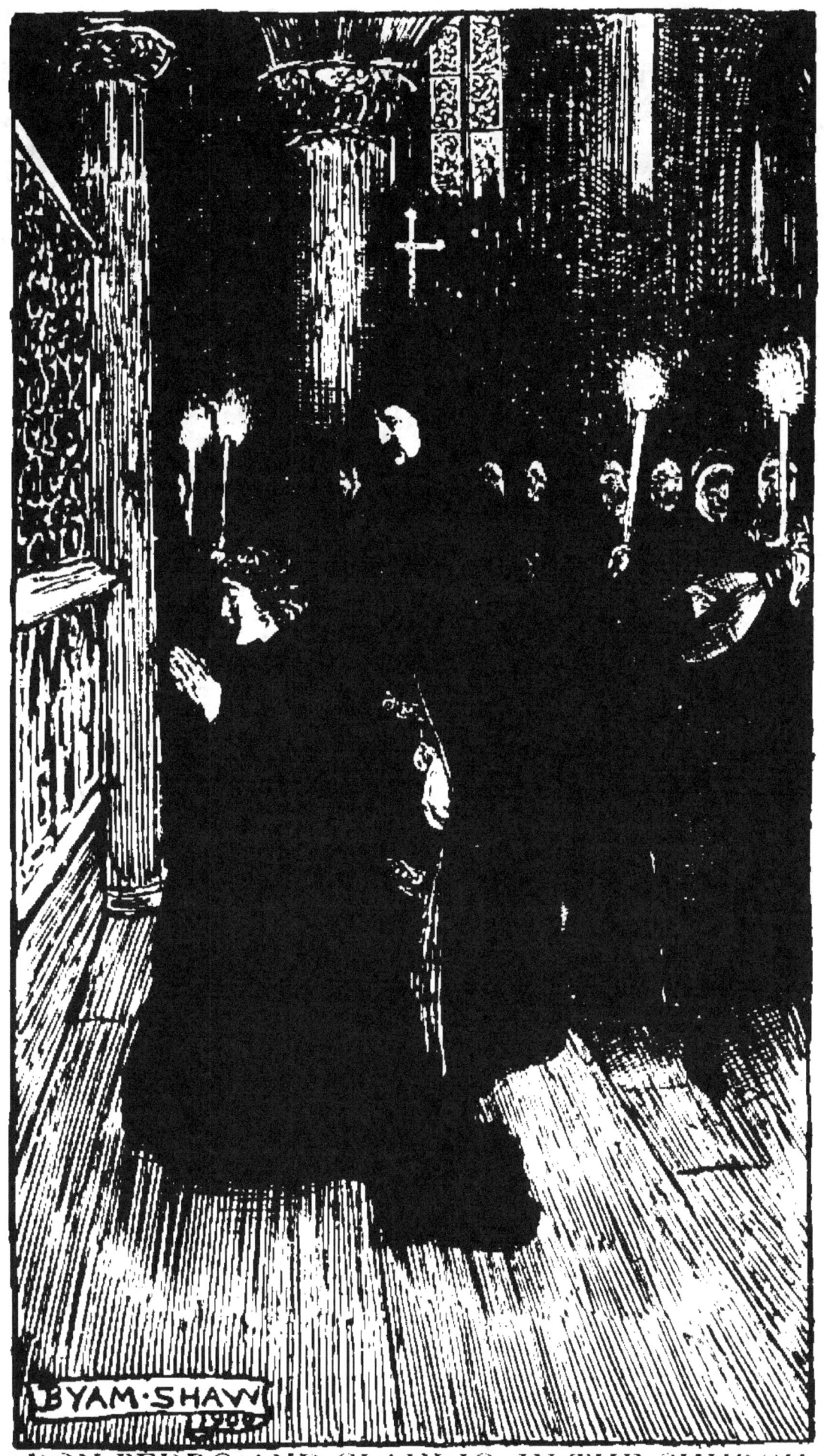

DON PEDRO AND CLAUDIO, IN THE CHURCH

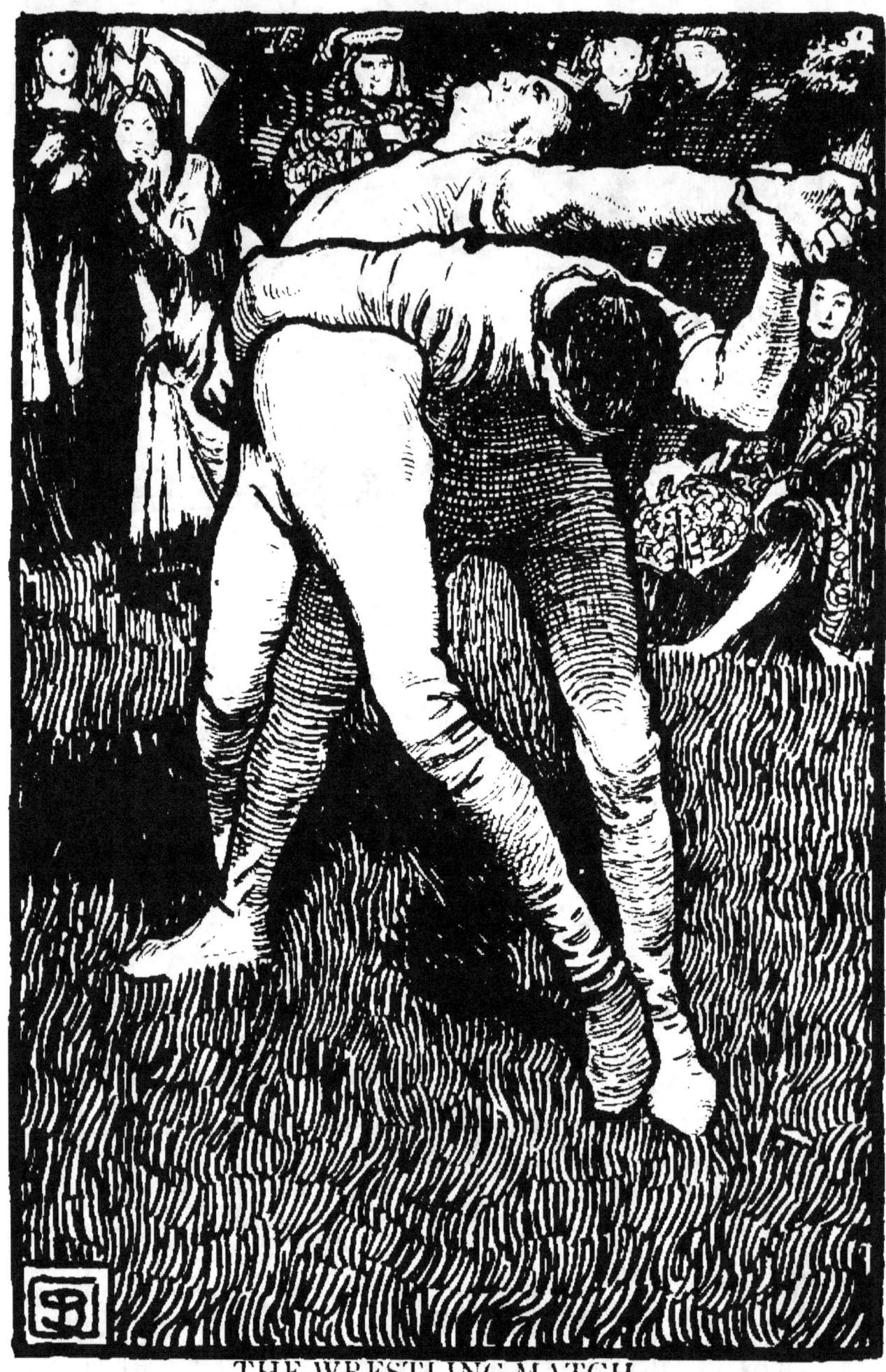

THE WRESTLING-MATCH.

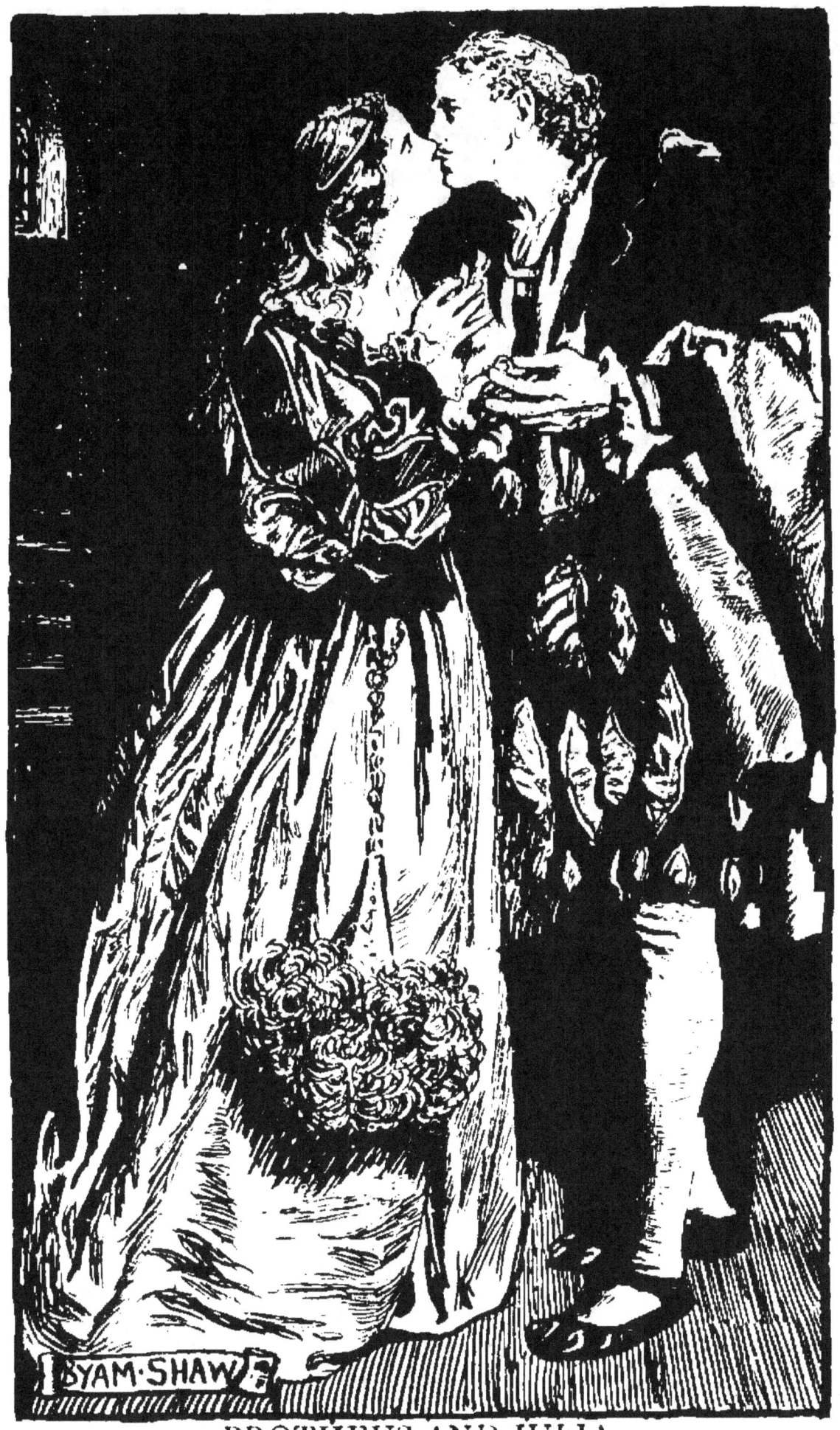

PROTHEUS AND JULIA

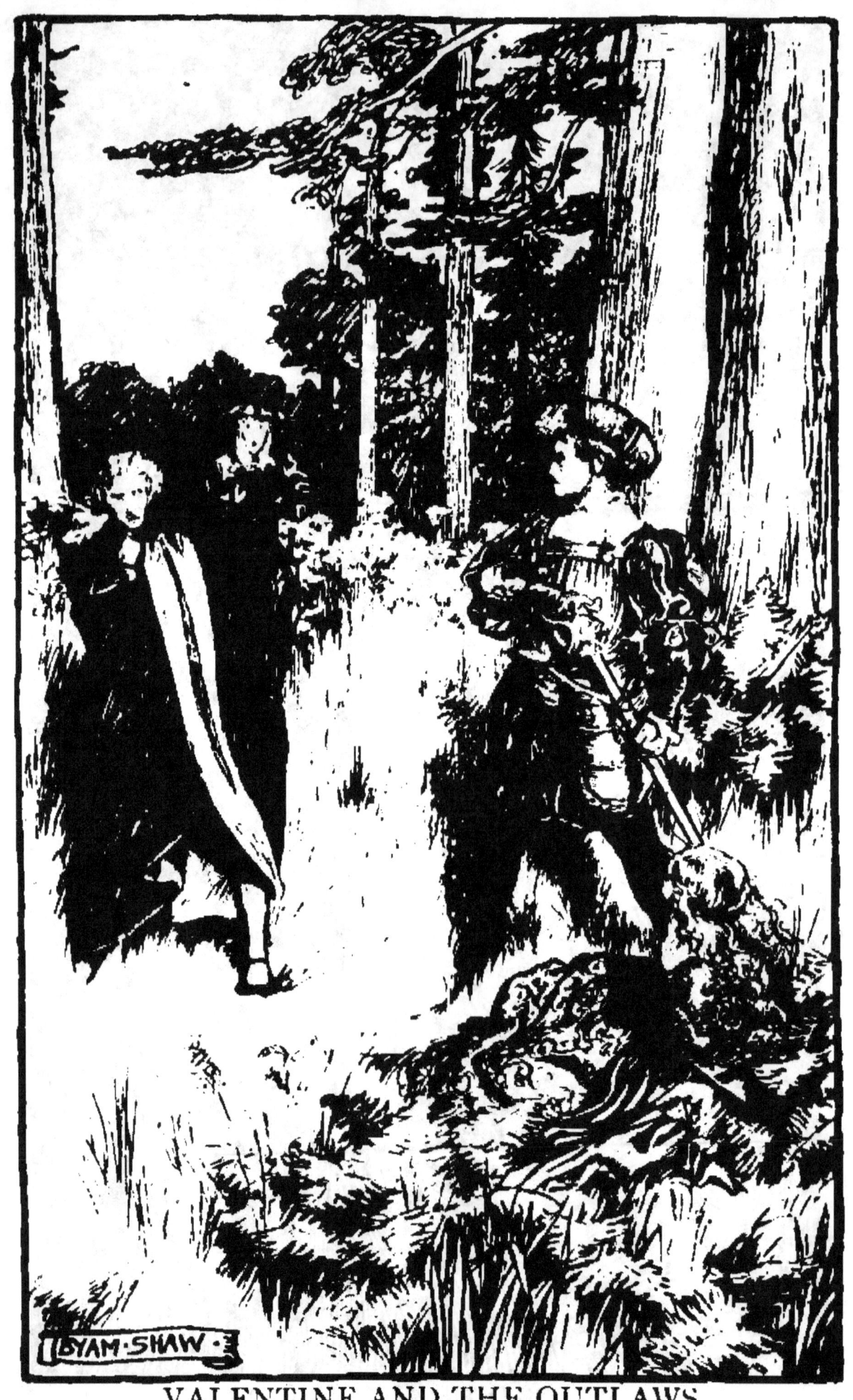

VALENTINE AND THE OUTLAWS.

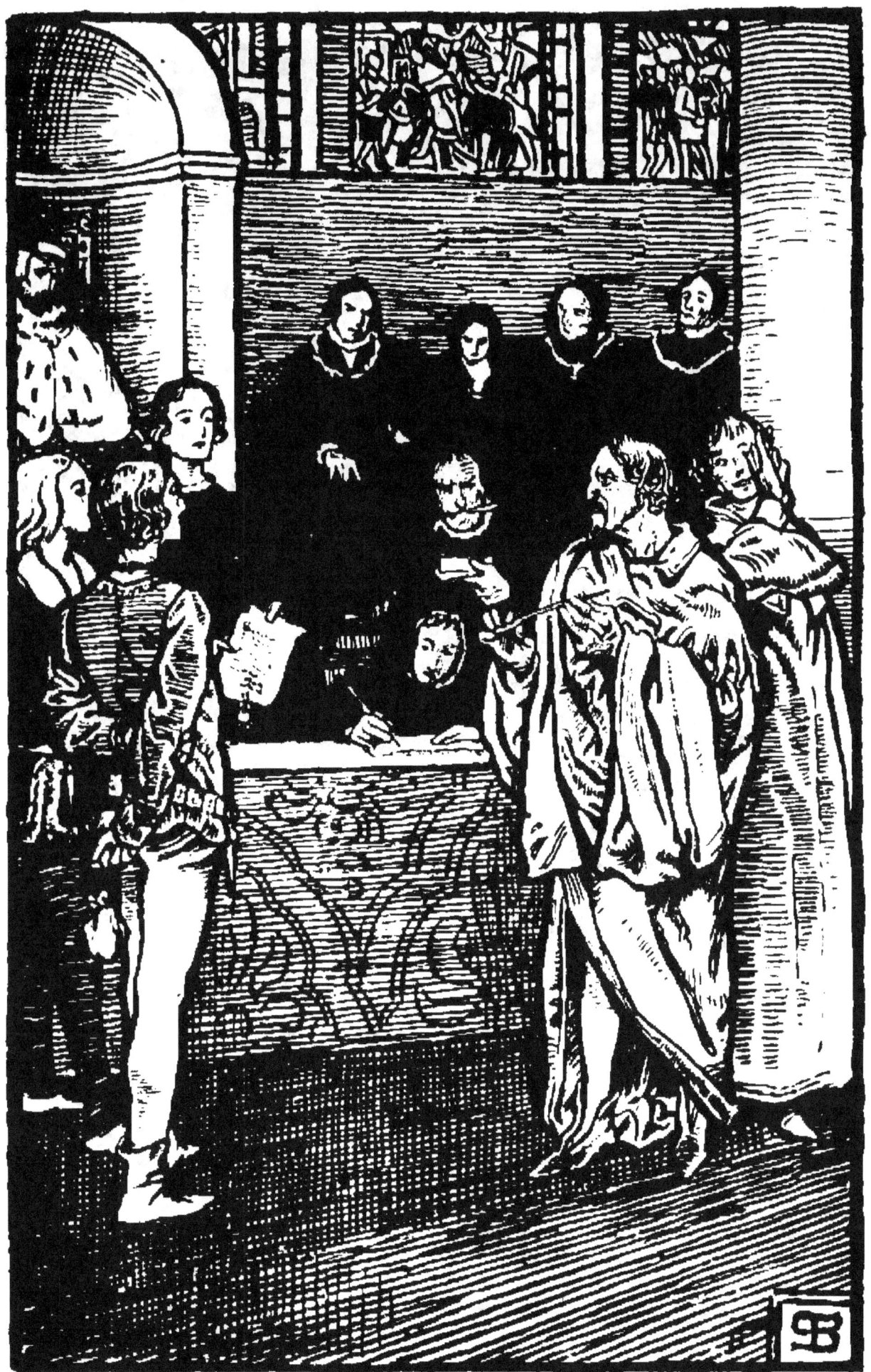

THE TRIAL.

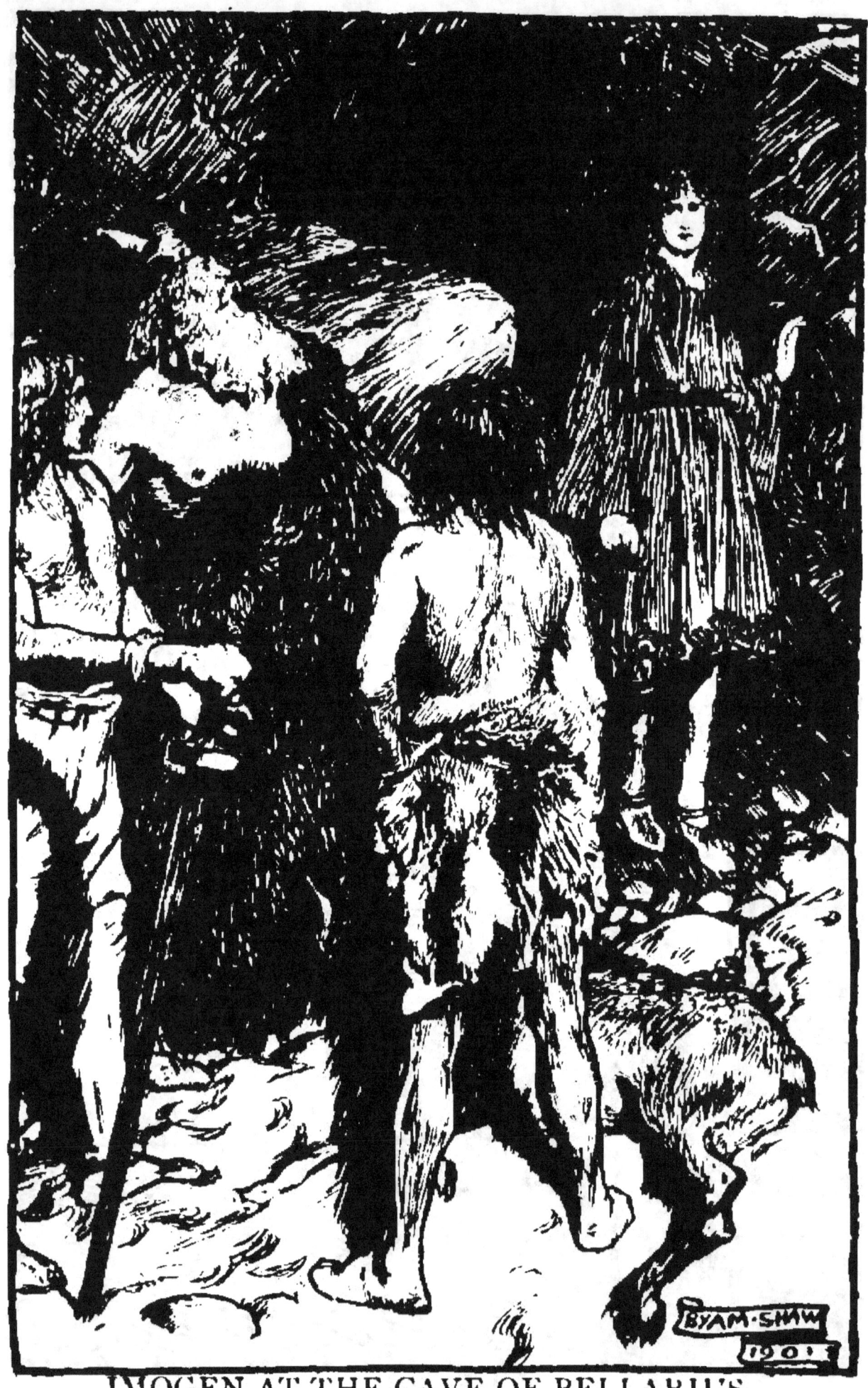

IMOGEN AT THE CAVE OF BELLARIUS.

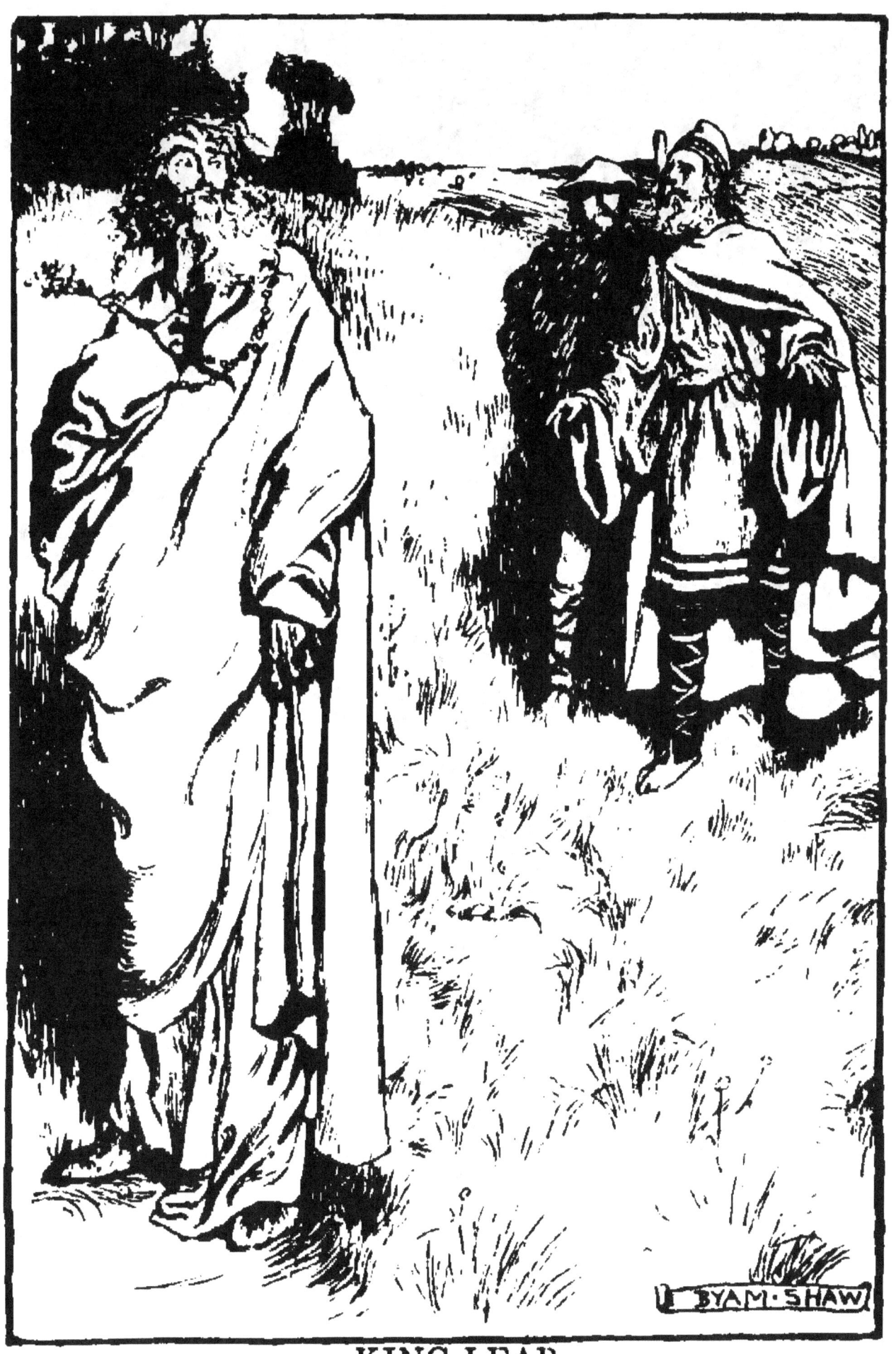

KING LEAR.
"AY EVERY INCH A KING."

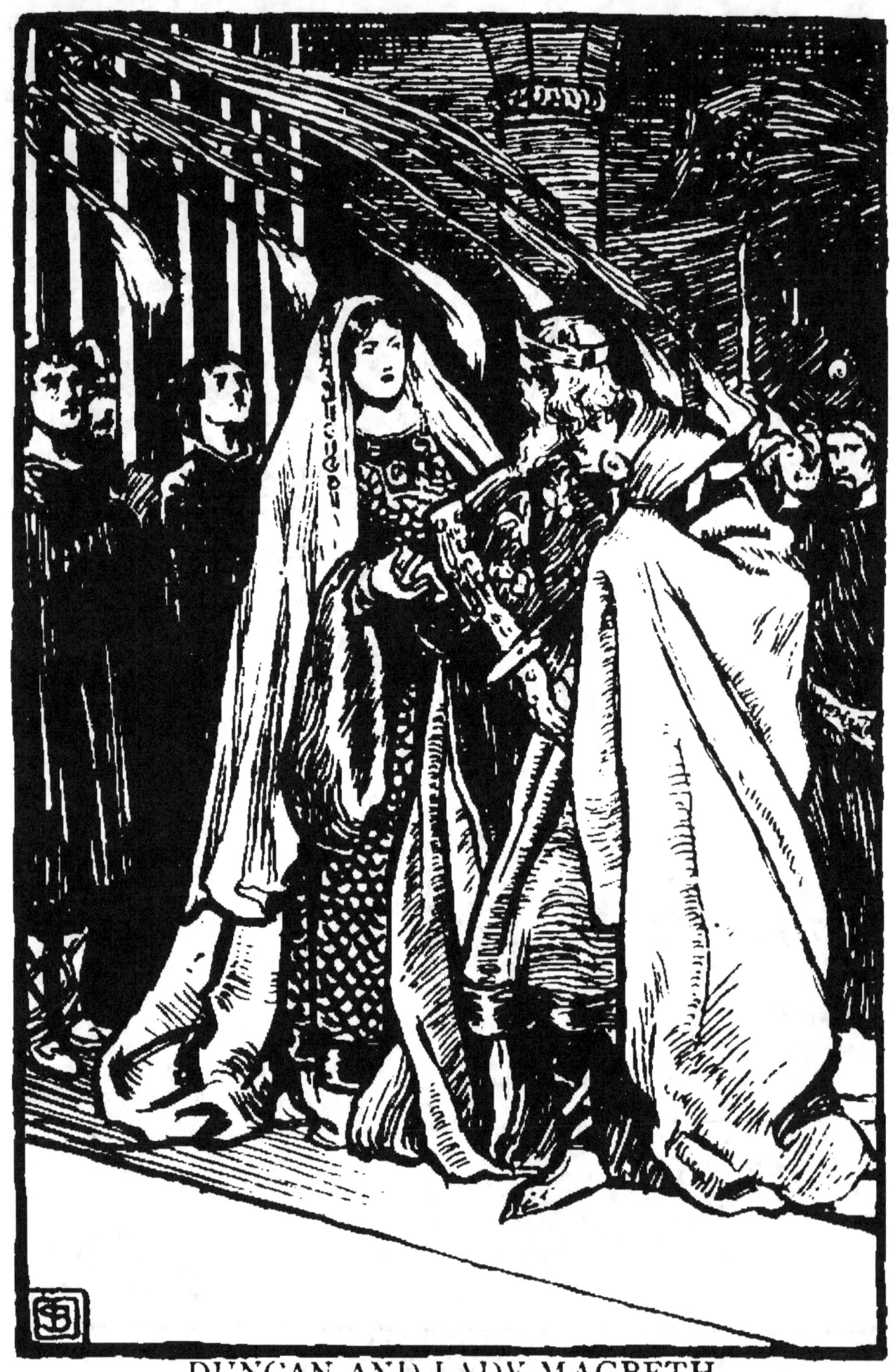

DUNCAN AND LADY MACBETH.

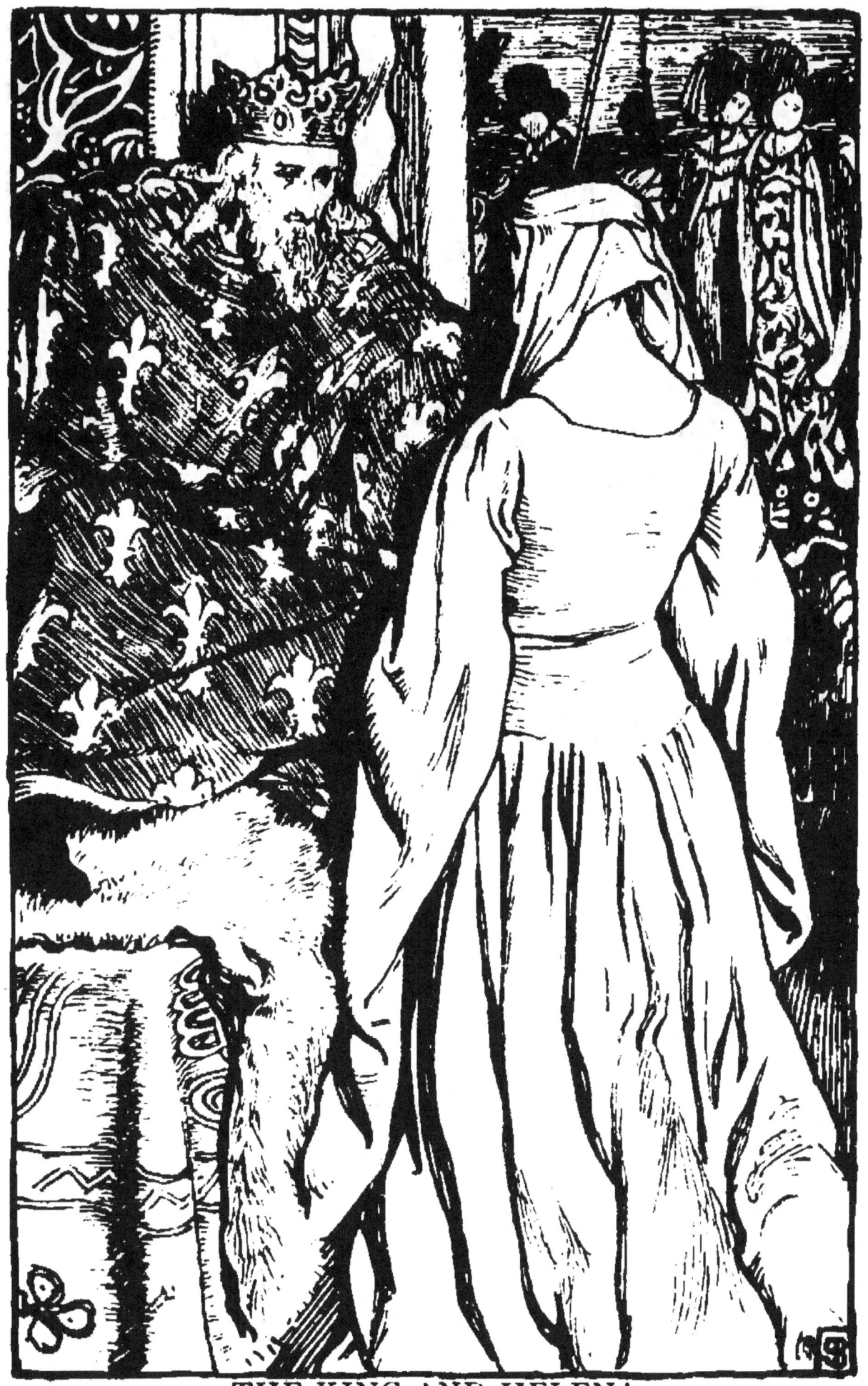

THE KING AND HELENA.

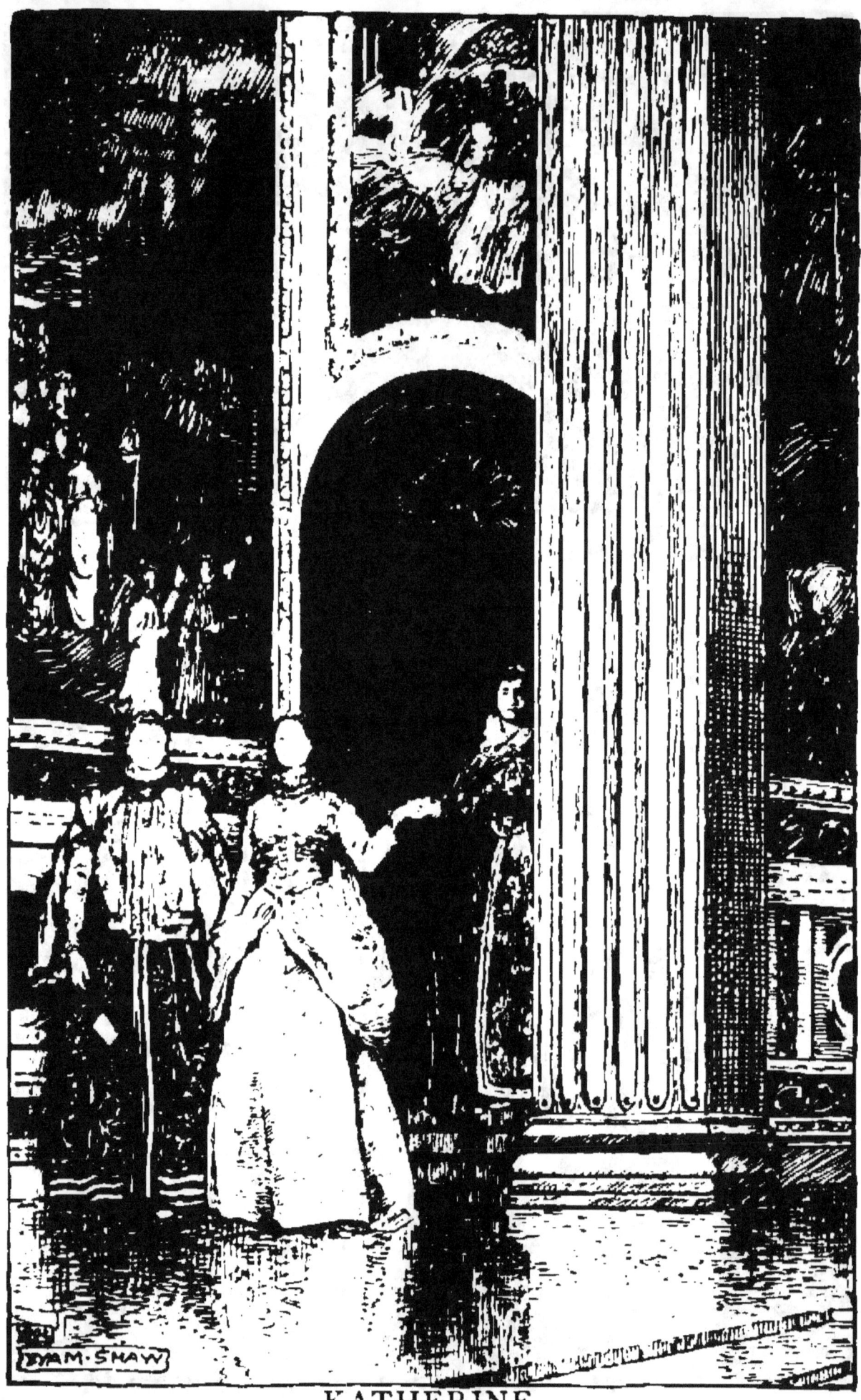

KATHERINE.

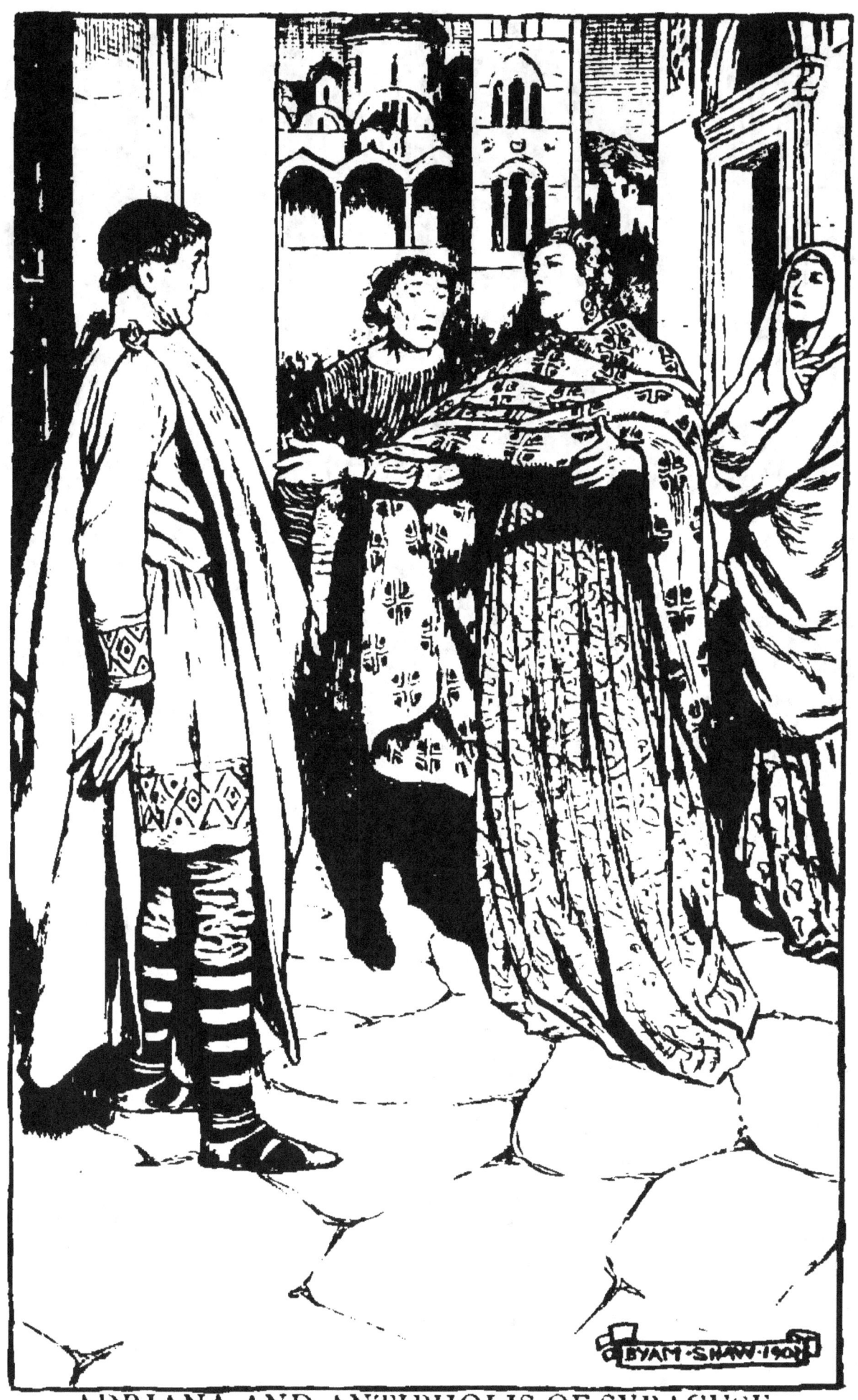

ADRIANA AND ANTIPHOLIS OF SYRACUSE.

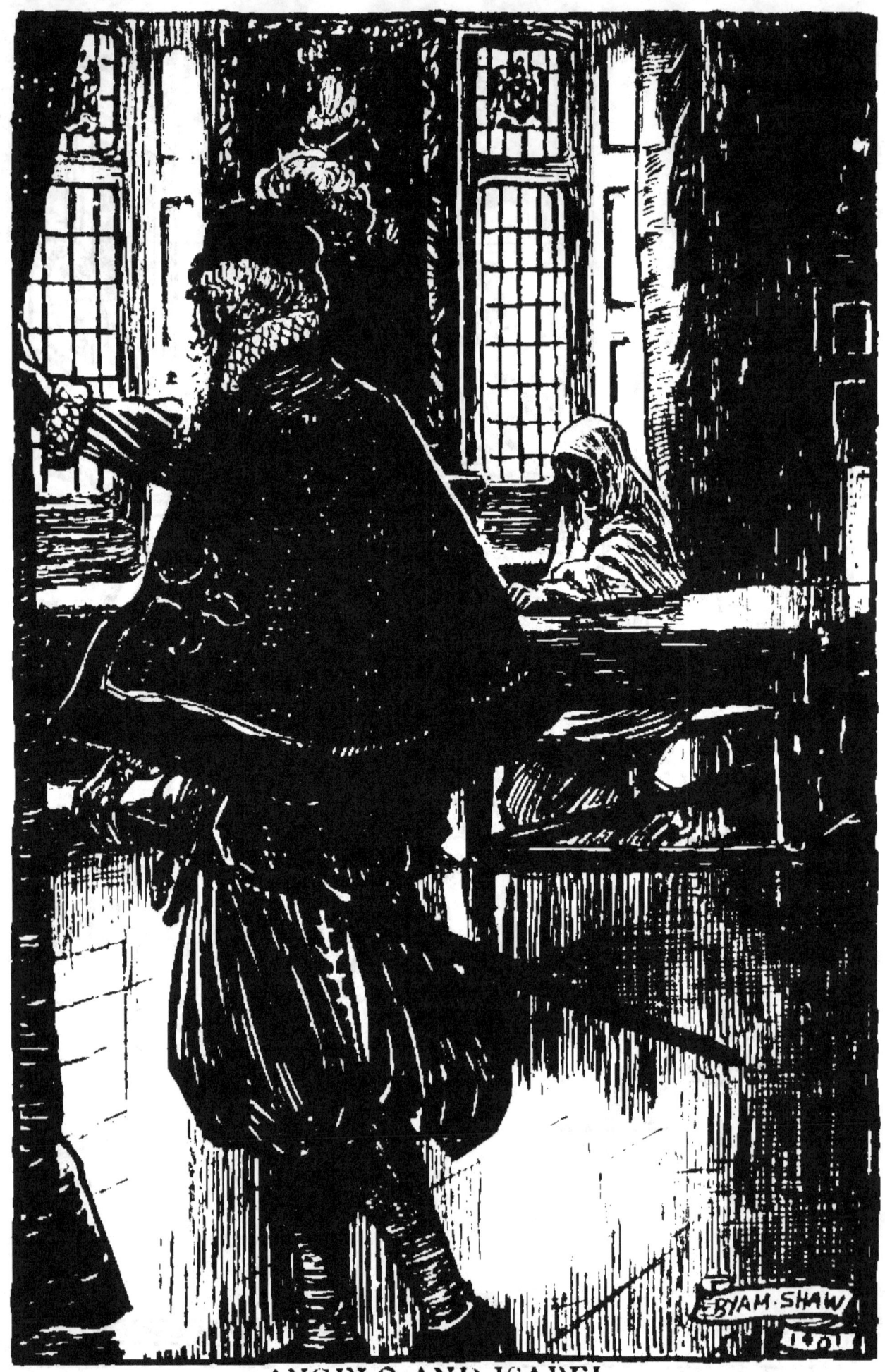

ANGELO AND ISABEL.

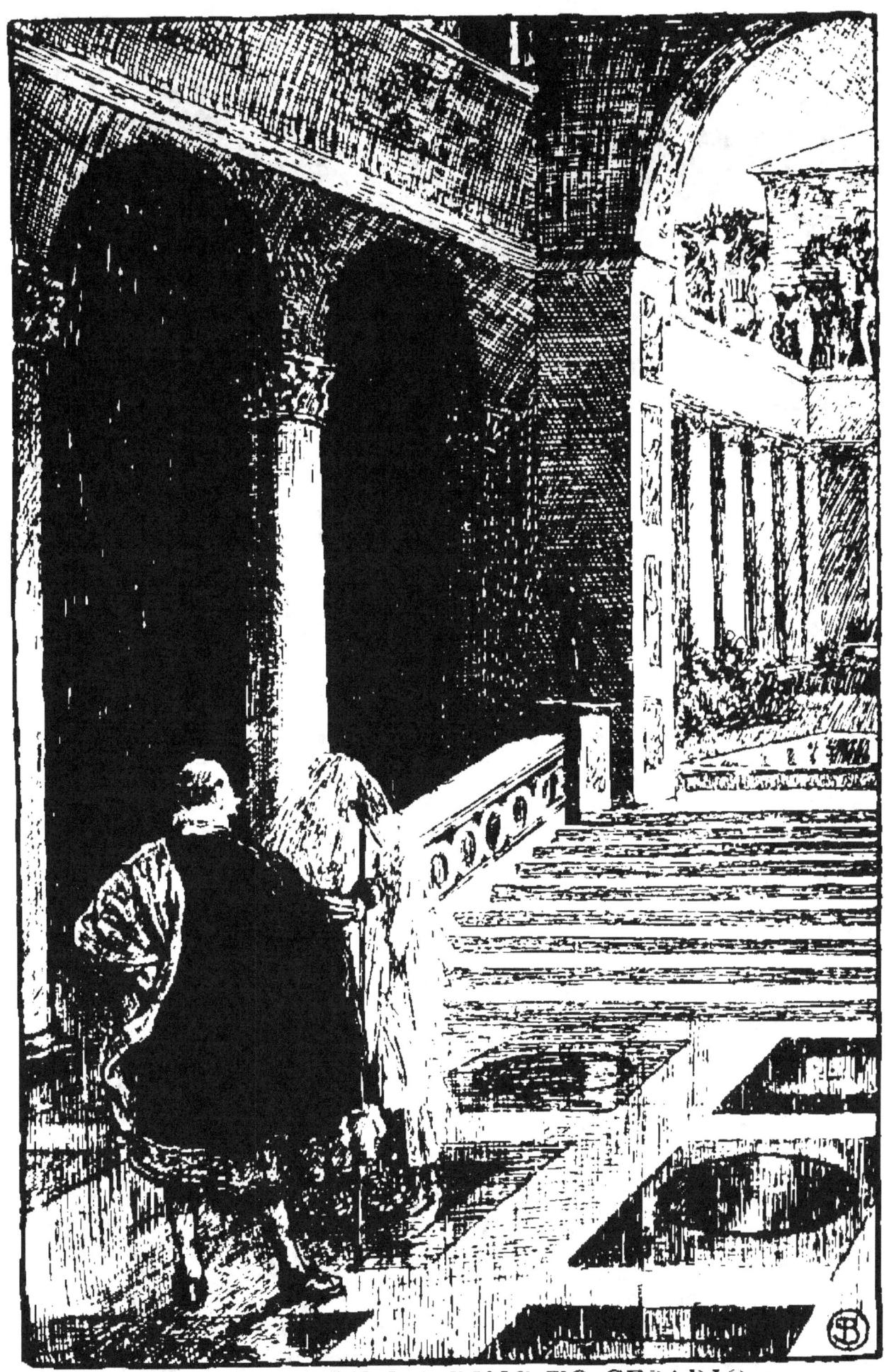

OLIVIA SENDS A RING TO CESARIO.

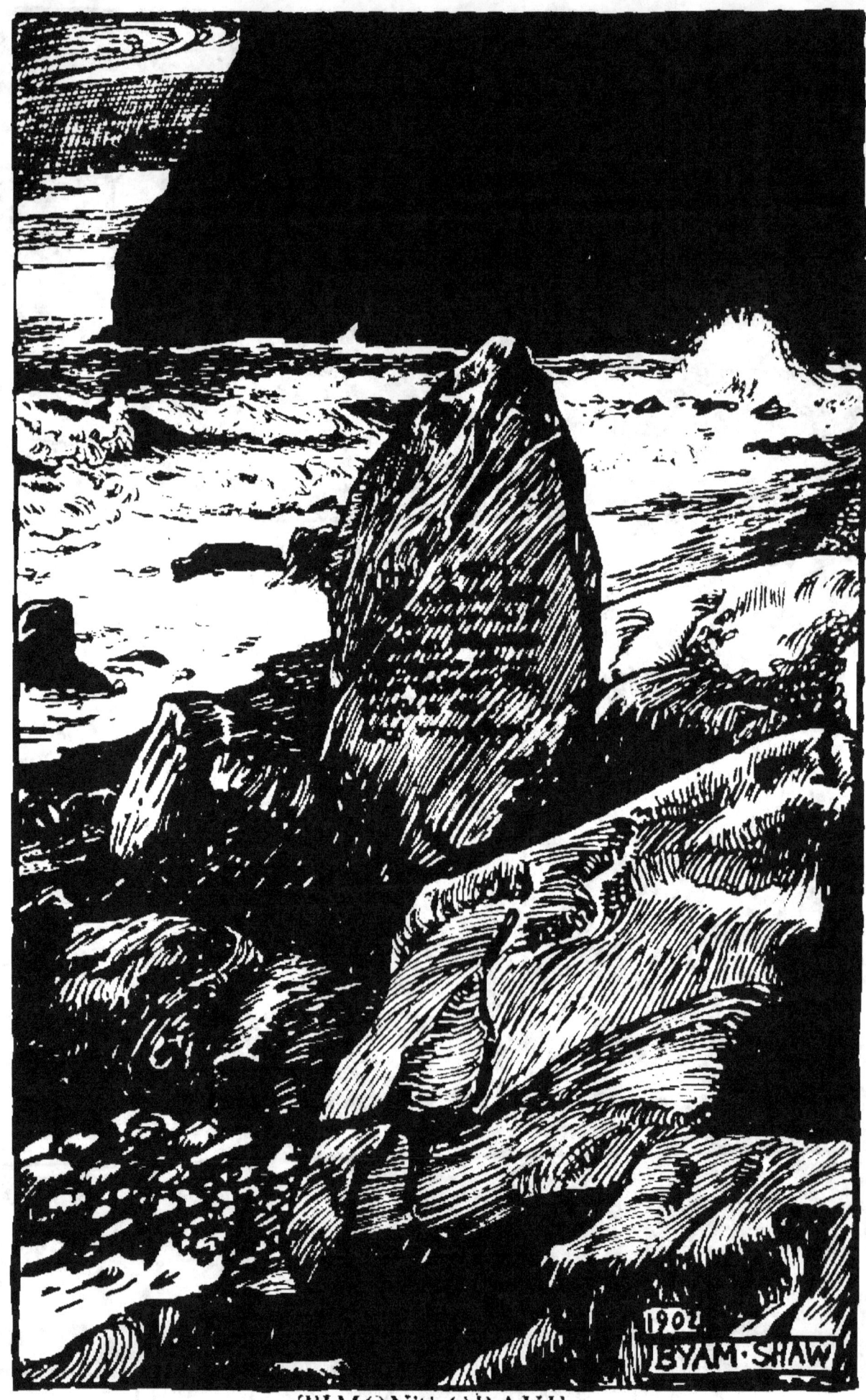

TIMON'S GRAVE.

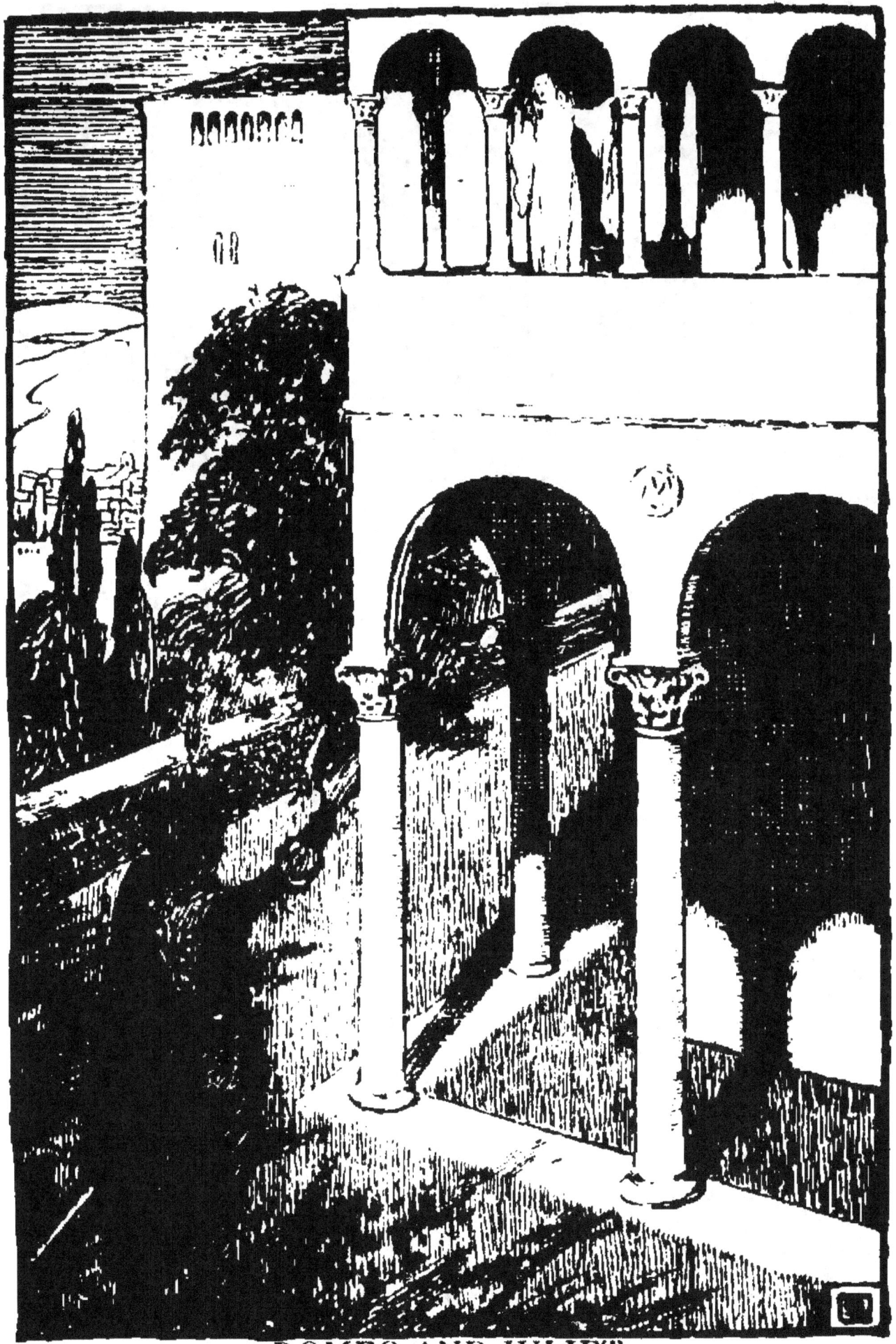

ROMEO AND JULIET.

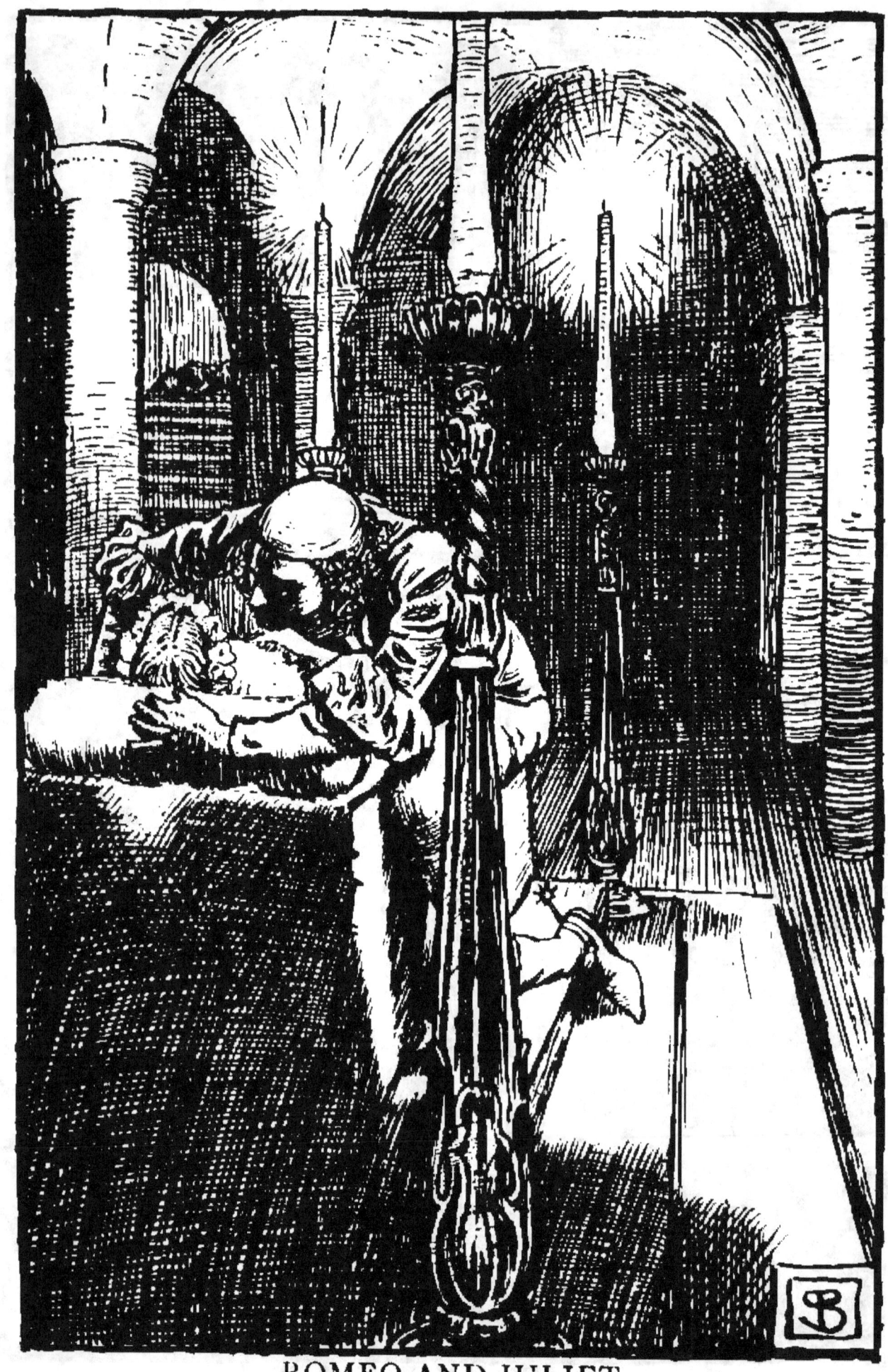

ROMEO AND JULIET.

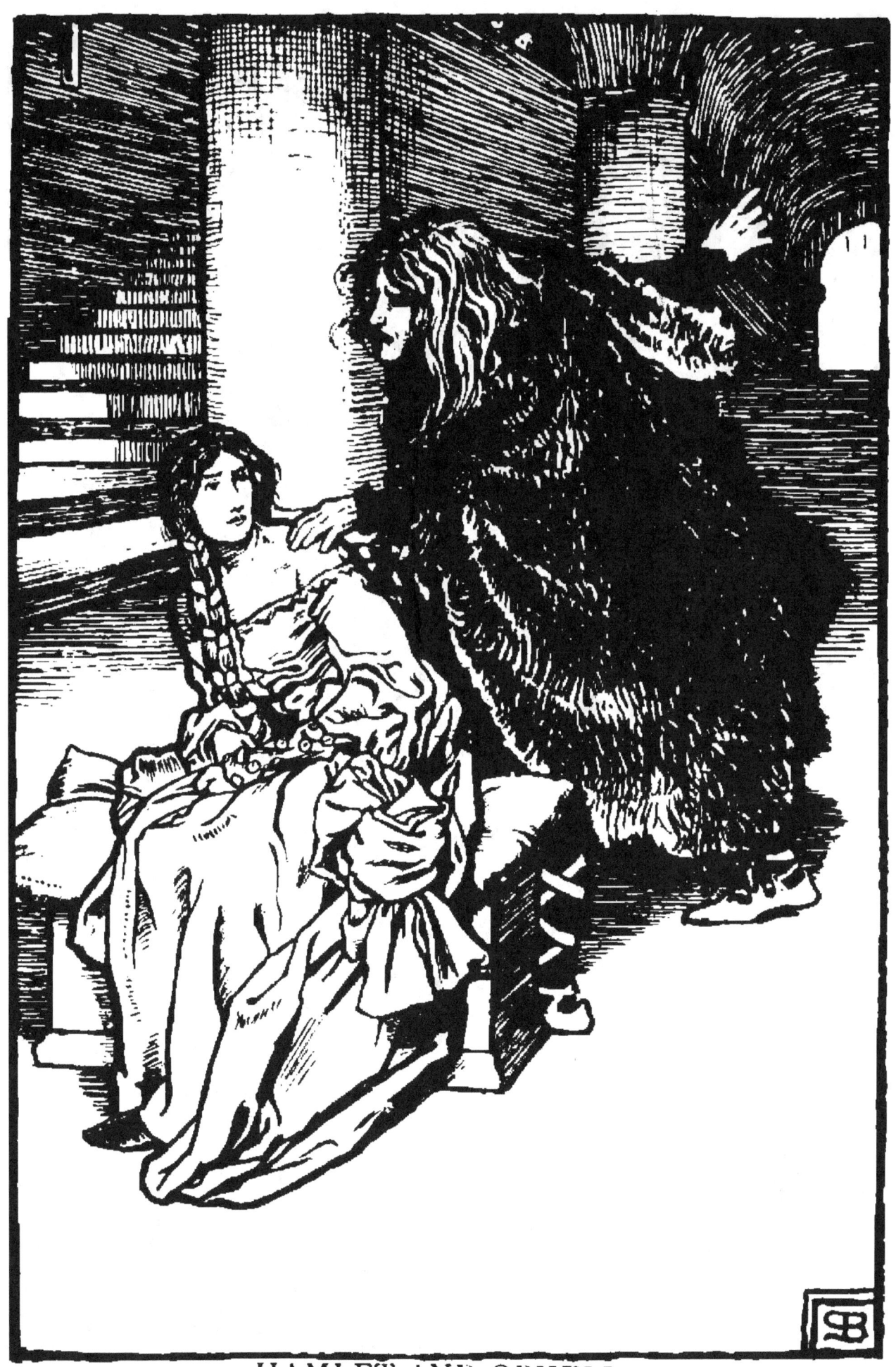

HAMLET AND OPHELIA.

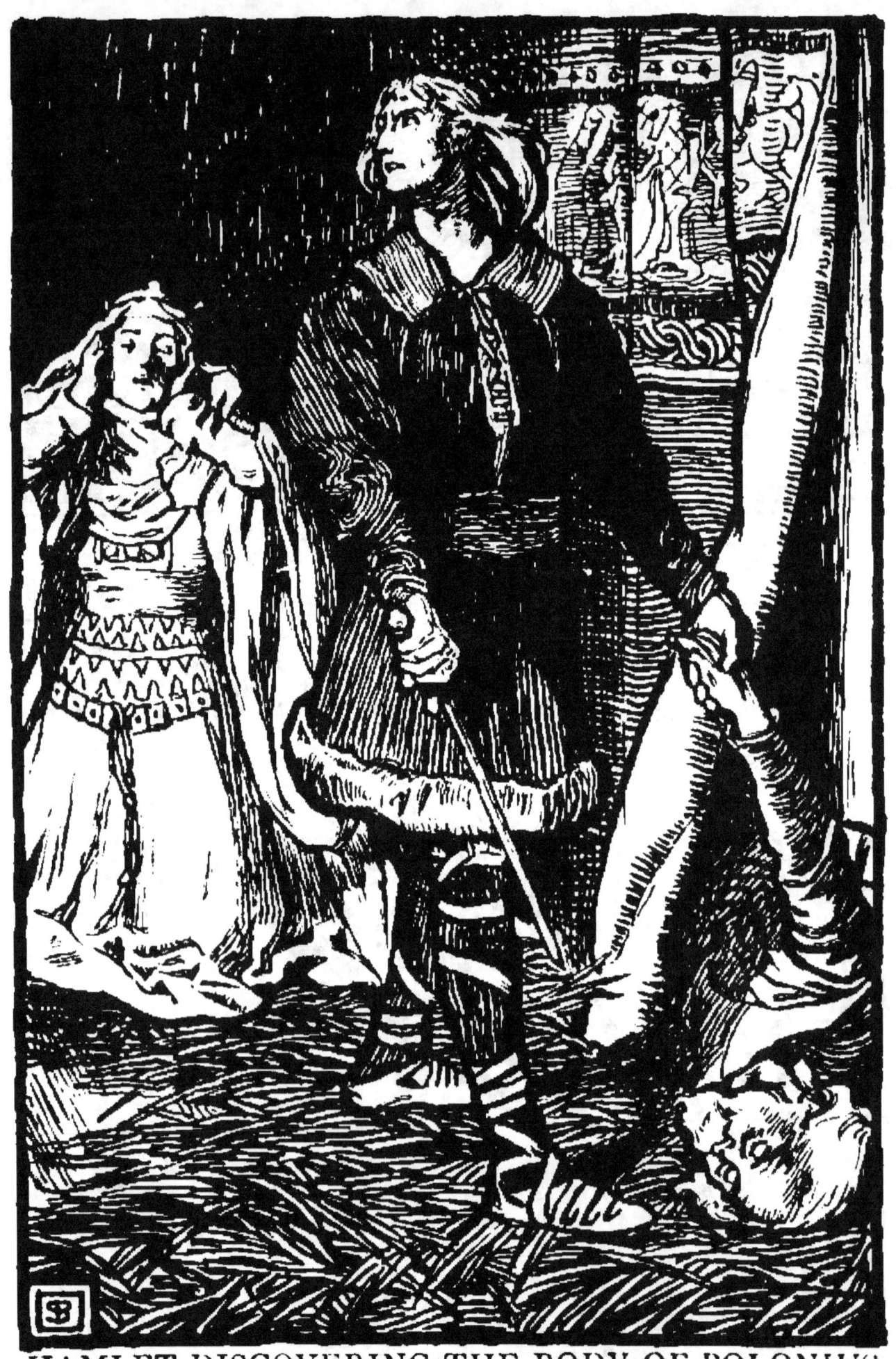

HAMLET DISCOVERING THE BODY OF POLONIUS.

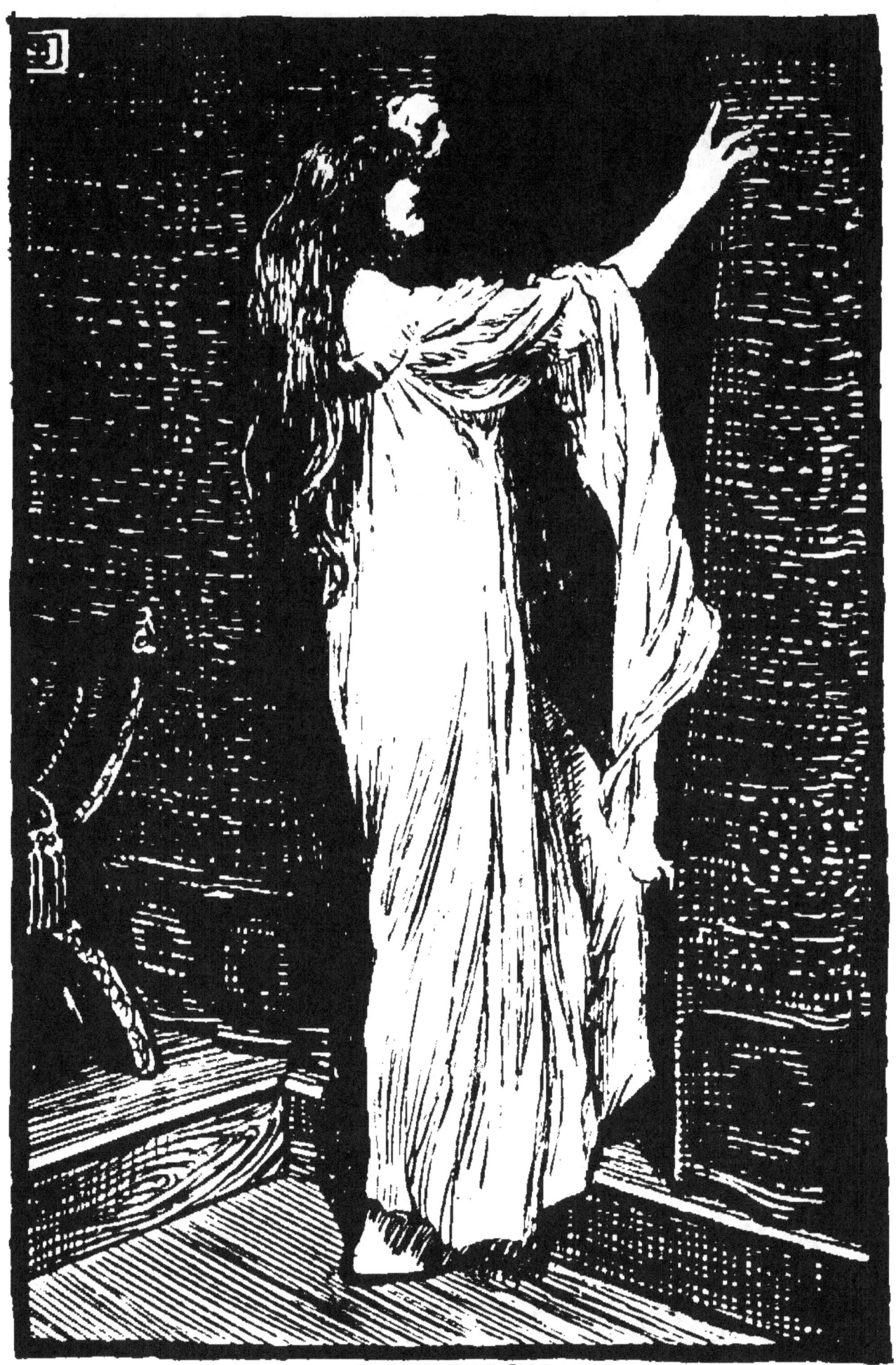

DESDEMONA.

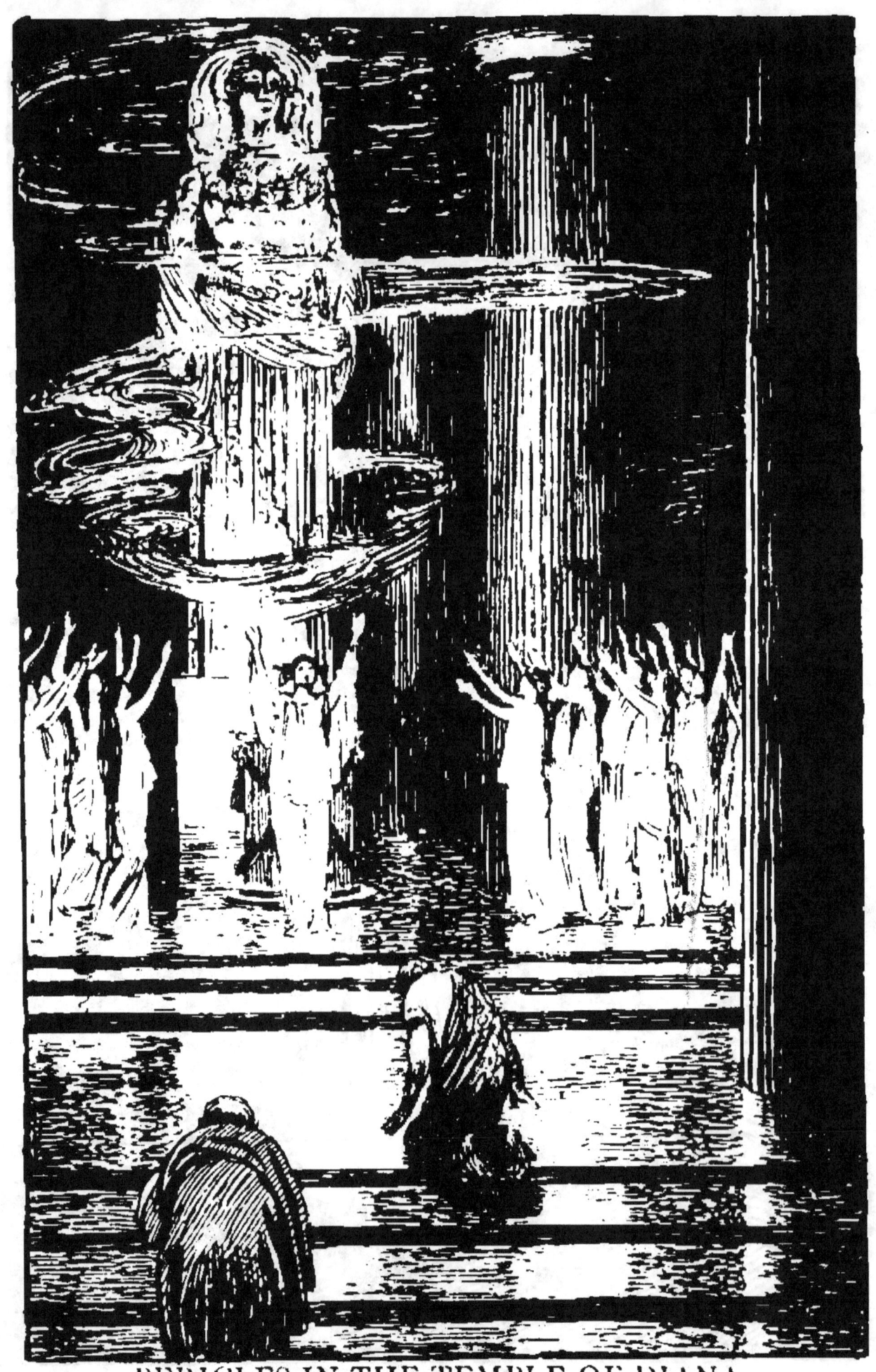

PERICLES IN THE TEMPLE OF DIANA.

www.ingramcontent.com/pod-product-compliance
Lightning Source LLC
Chambersburg PA
CBHW081625220526
45468CB00010B/3028